Let's Make
MUSIC

The Recorder

and other wind instruments

Rita Storey

FRANKLIN WATTS

LONDON • SYDNEY

First published in 2007 by
Franklin Watts
338 Euston Road
London NW1 3BH

Franklin Watts Australia
Level 17/207 Kent Street
Sydney NSW 2000

Art director: Jonathan Hair
Series designed and created for Franklin Watts by Painted Fish Ltd.
Designer: Rita Storey
Editor: Fiona Corbridge
Adviser: Helen MacGregor

Picture credits
istockphoto.com pp. 4, 5, 8, 15 (bottom),16, 17 (top right and bottom), 18, 20, 21
(bottom), 25, 26 (top left and top right); Mick Hudson/ Redferns p. 26 (bottom);
Tudor Photography pp. 3, 6, 7, 9, 10, 11, 12, 13, 14, 15 (top), 17 (top left), 19, 21
(top), 22, 23; CBSO/ Adrian Burrows p. 24.

Cover images: Tudor Photography, Banbury (top, middle and bottom right);
istock.com (bottom left, far left and far right).

All photos posed by models.
Thanks to Husnen Ahmad, James Barlow, Jo Cox, Maddi Indun, Stephen Morris
and Natasha Vinall.

ISBN 978 0 7496 7581 3

Dewey classification: 788

A CIP catalogue record for this book is available from the British Library.

Printed in China

Frankin Watts is a division of Hachette Children's Books, an Hachette Livre UK
company.

Contents

Words in **bold** are in the glossary.

The recorder

Musical instruments that you blow are called wind instruments. A recorder is a wind instrument.

The recorder is part of a family of wind instruments called **woodwind** instruments.

This girl is playing a recorder.

Making a sound

To make a sound with a recorder, you blow through the mouthpiece.

Changing the sound

To change the sound, or musical note, that comes out of the recorder, you cover different holes with your fingers.

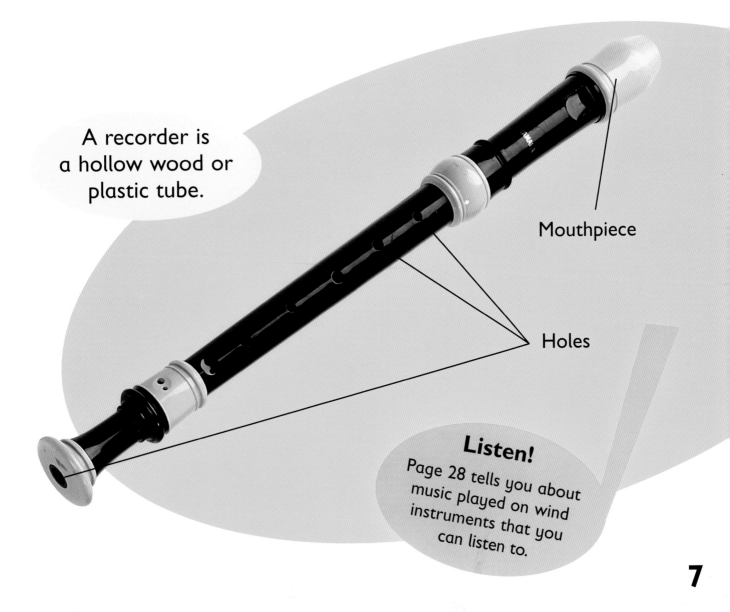

A recorder is a hollow wood or plastic tube.

Mouthpiece

Holes

Listen!
Page 28 tells you about music played on wind instruments that you can listen to.

The sound

When you blow into a recorder, the air splits up and goes in different directions.

Where the air goes

Some of the air comes out through a hole called the fipple. The rest of it goes down the recorder and then out through the fingerholes and the hole in the bottom of the foot.

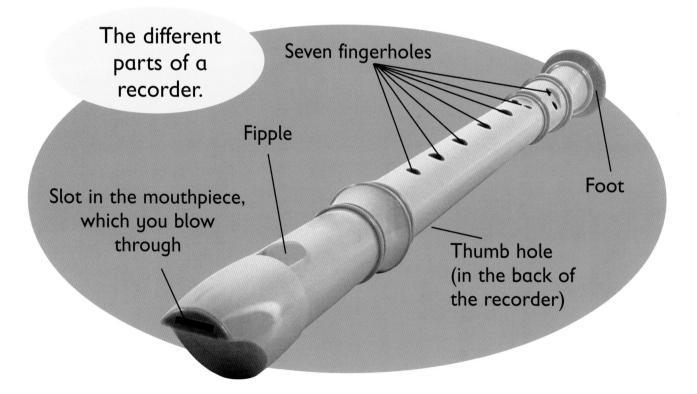

The different parts of a recorder.

Seven fingerholes

Fipple

Foot

Slot in the mouthpiece, which you blow through

Thumb hole (in the back of the recorder)

Sound waves

When the air splits, it wobbles very fast. The air is **vibrating**. These vibrations in the air are called **sound waves**.

Try this

Blow across the top of a plastic bottle. Some of the air will go into the bottle and some will go across the outside. Can you hear a noise? Sound waves make the sound that you hear.

Musical notes

You can make different sounds, or musical notes, on a recorder.

High and low

Some sounds are high and some are low.
We say they have a high **pitch** or a low pitch.

There are different sizes of recorder. Each one has a different overall sound, or pitch. The length and width of a recorder affect its pitch.

A descant recorder has a short, narrow tube and the highest pitch

Treble recorder

Tenor recorder

A bass recorder has a long, wide tube and the lowest pitch

Playing notes

To play low notes, cover a lot of the holes with your fingers. To play high notes, cover just a few holes.

You only need to blow gently to make a sound. You move the tip of your tongue to play the rhythms.

Music notes

To be able to play music that other people have made up, or composed, you need to understand how to read music.

Music is written in musical notes. There are **symbols** to tell us how long or short a note is. The length of the notes make up the **rhythm** of a piece of music.

The notes are written on five lines called a stave. The place of a note on the stave tells us how high or low it is. This is called its pitch.

Long note   Short notes

This long note lasts for the same time as all the short notes put together.

Playing a low note.

Playing a high note.

11

Breathing

Controlling the way you breathe is very important when you play a wind instrument.

Your breath is the power that makes the sound. You need to be able to breathe deeply and evenly, so that you can play a lot of notes without gasping for air.

This girl is playing a long note on a flute.

Try this

Take a deep breath and breathe out quickly – as if you were blowing out a candle.

Take a deep breath and breathe out as slowly and evenly as you can. Time yourself. Can you breathe out even more slowly?

The flute

The flute is part of the woodwind instrument family. You play it by blowing *across* the mouthpiece. This has a hole in it that goes into the tube.

As you blow, some of the air goes into the hole and some goes over it. This makes the air in the tube vibrate and creates a sound.

Playing a flute.

Mouthpiece

Flutes are usually made of metal. They are longer than a recorder. Some are made in three parts that have to be fitted together.

A piccolo is a small flute. It is shorter than a flute and plays higher notes.

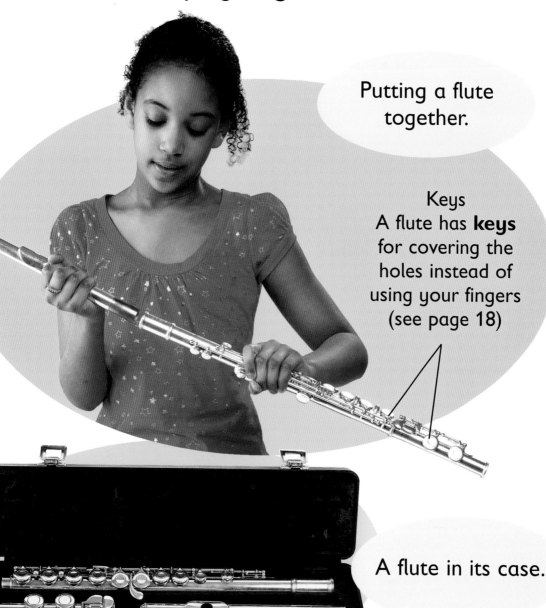

Putting a flute together.

Keys
A flute has **keys** for covering the holes instead of using your fingers (see page 18)

A flute in its case.

Oboe and clarinet

Other woodwind instruments are played in different ways.

Reeds

Oboes and clarinets have a mouthpiece with one or two thin pieces of wood or plastic called a reed. When you blow into the mouthpiece, the reed vibrates.

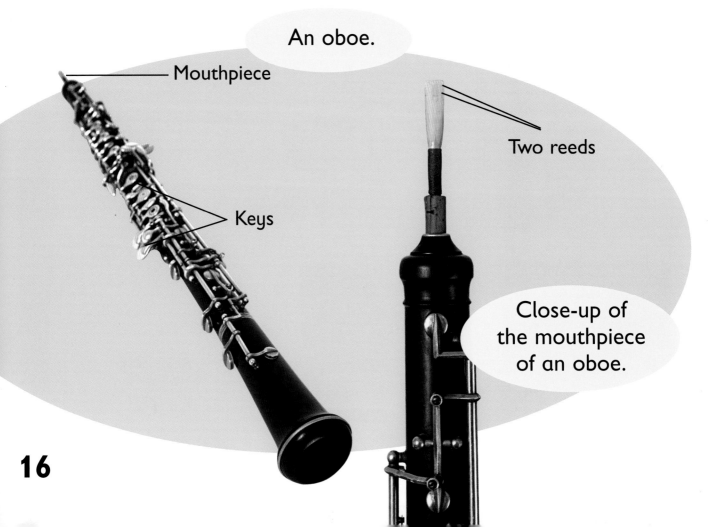

An oboe.

Mouthpiece

Keys

Two reeds

Close-up of the mouthpiece of an oboe.

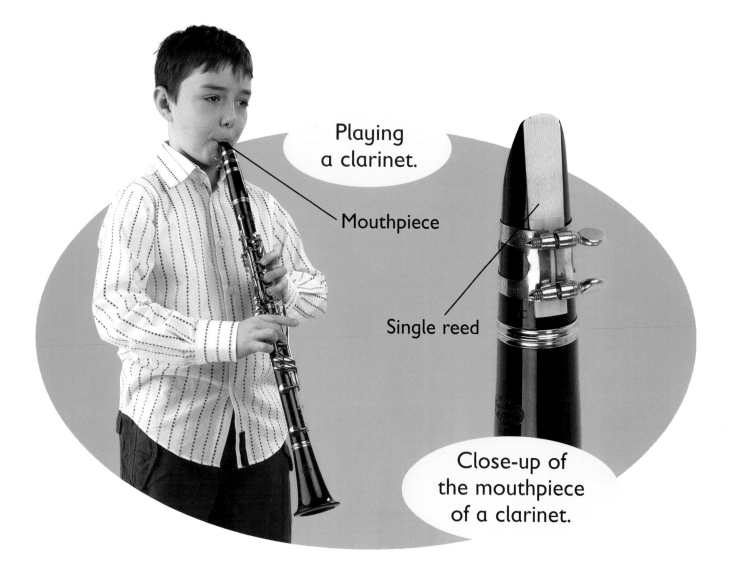

Playing a clarinet.

Mouthpiece

Single reed

Close-up of the mouthpiece of a clarinet.

Making a sound

The vibrating reeds make the air in the tube vibrate, and this makes the sound.

Instruments with reeds can be heard clearly even when there is a large group of instruments playing together.

Music notes

Not all woodwind instruments are made of wood.
This saxophone is part of the woodwind family. It is made of metal and has reeds in its mouthpiece.

17

Closing the holes

Some wind instruments have a long tube, and it is hard to reach all the holes with our fingers. These long instruments make low-pitched sounds.

Using levers

Instead of using your fingers to cover the holes on a long wind instrument, you press **levers** that push padded **keys** over the holes.

Playing a clarinet using the levers.

A lot of notes

Levers allow you to press down groups of
keys at the same time. By using levers as well
as your fingers, you can play a lot of different
notes on these
instruments.

Saxophones have
a lot of levers.

Brass

Another group of wind instruments are the brass instruments. These are made of metal tubes. The trumpet, trombone and French horn are in this group.

The metal tube of each instrument is a different length and shape. It flares out at the end into a bell shape. The longer the tube is, the lower the pitch of the notes it makes.

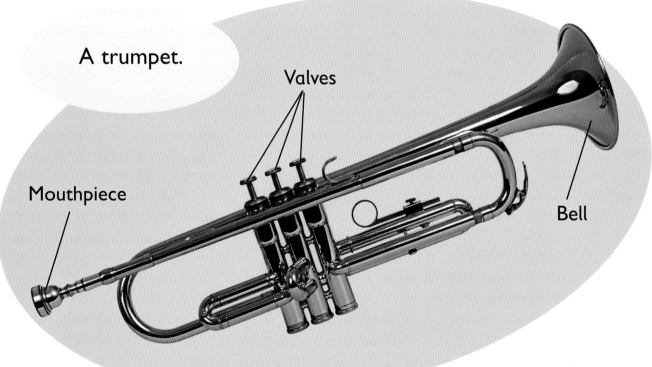

A trumpet.

Valves

Mouthpiece

Bell

Slides and valves

On a trombone, you can make the tube longer or shorter by closing the holes with **valves** or by using the **slide**.

Slide

Playing a trombone using the slide.

Bending the tube

To make them easier to hold, the tubes of brass instruments are **coiled**. This French horn has over 4 metres of coiled tubing.

Playing brass

When you play a brass instrument, you use your lips and tongue to change the sounds it makes.

Changing the sound

If you make your lips vibrate against the mouthpiece when you blow, it is called 'buzzing'. If you change the shape you make with your lips, it changes the sound of the notes.

Make this shape with your lips and blow. Can you make a buzzing sound?

Tonguing

'Tonguing' is a word used to describe the position of your tongue inside your mouth when you play.

The position of your tongue affects the pitch of the notes. If your tongue is high in your mouth, a note will have a higher pitch than if your tongue is low in your mouth.

All together

Different wind instruments are often played together.

Recorders do not make a very loud sound, but sometimes they may be played as part of a small group of musicians called a chamber orchestra.

Wind instruments that make a louder sound are played in larger **orchestras**.

Playing the contra bassoon in an orchestra. It has a very low pitch.

These students are playing saxophones in a jazz band.

Jazz bands

Saxophones, trombones, trumpets and clarinets are used to play **jazz** music in big bands.

Brass bands

Brass instruments are played together in brass bands and **marching bands**.

Music notes

The way that a piece of music is played is called its **mood**.
The speed at which a piece of music is played is called its **tempo**.

Blown away

Many different types of wind instruments are played in countries all over the world. Here are just a few of them.

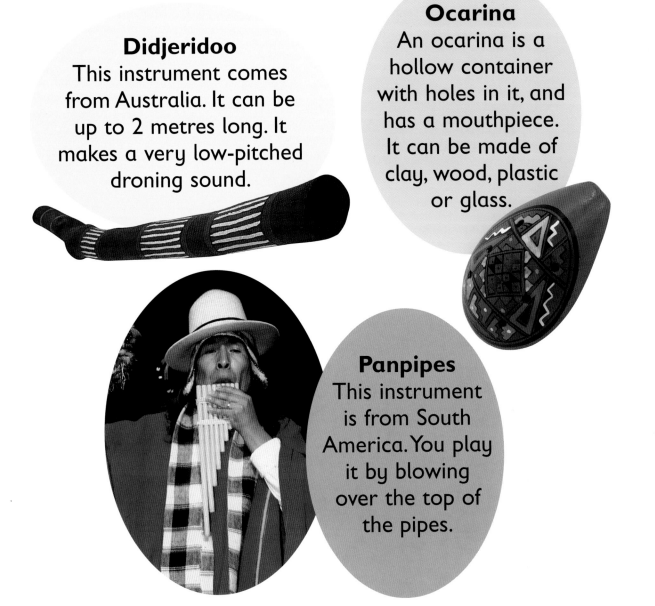

Didjeridoo
This instrument comes from Australia. It can be up to 2 metres long. It makes a very low-pitched droning sound.

Ocarina
An ocarina is a hollow container with holes in it, and has a mouthpiece. It can be made of clay, wood, plastic or glass.

Panpipes
This instrument is from South America. You play it by blowing over the top of the pipes.

Listen!

Websites

Recorder

Find out about the recorder and how to play popular children's tunes at:
http://www.bbc.co.uk/dna/h2g2/A506387

Do you want to learn the notes on a descant recorder? Use the interactive fingering chart at:
http://www.dolmetsch.com/cfingerchart.htm

Visit the recorder player's page on this site to hear lots of different styles of recorder music and download music:
http://www.saers.com/recorder/

Other wind instruments

See and hear the whole range of wind and brass instruments by clicking on the trumpet at:
http://ngfl.northumberland.gov.uk/music/orchestra/default.htm

Explore the orchestra with the New York Philharmonic at:
www.nyphilkids.org
Walk through the instrument storage room to read about woodwind and brass instruments, and listen to music for each instrument.

Make your own set of panpipes – go to:
http://library.thinkquest.org/5116/pan_pipes.htm

Read about bagpipes and their history at:
http://www.bbc.co.uk/dna/h2g2/A748208

See different ocarinas and learn how to make one from clay at:
http://www.bbc.co.uk/dna/h2g2/A1090649

Look at this Australian site for lots of information about the didgeridoo and how it is played:
http://www.aboriginalart.com.au/didgeridoo/trad.html

CDs

Listen to these well-known pieces of music
on the recorder and other wind instruments:

Vivaldi: *Recorder Concert in C.*

Britten: *Young Person's Guide to the Orchestra.*

Prokofiev: *Peter and the Wolf.* (Woodwind instruments represent the main characters in the story. The clarinet is the cat, the bassoon is the grandfather, and the flute is the bird.)

Saint-Saëns: *Carnival of the Animals.* (The flute represents an aviary.)

Glen Miller: *Tuxedo Junction* (brass and woodwind).

El Condor Pasa: *Music of the Andes* (flutes and panpipes).

Rough Guide to Aboriginal Music (didgeridoo).

Glossary

Coiled Wound round and round.

Jazz A style of music that began in New Orleans, USA.

Keys Pads attached to metal levers. They are used to open and close holes.

Lever A bar that you press down at one end to make the other end go up.

Marching band A group of musicians who play instruments while marching along.

Mood The way that a piece of music is played.

Orchestra A large group of performers playing various musical instruments.

Pitch A high musical note or sound is said to have a high pitch. A low musical note or sound is said to have a low pitch.

Rhythm The regular pattern of sound in music.

Slide A part of a trombone, which you can move backwards and forwards to change the pitch of a note.

Sound wave A wave that transmits sound through the air.

Symbol A shape used to represent something else.

Tempo The speed at which music is played.

Valves In a trumpet and a trombone, these change the length of the column of air in the instrument to alter pitch.

Vibrating; vibration Moving backwards and forwards, or up and down, quickly; this movement.

Woodwind A group of wind instruments played using reeds in the mouthpiece. This group also includes the flute.

Index